Need to Know
Alcohol

Sean Connolly

Heinemann
LIBRARY

www.heinemann.co.uk
visit our website to find out more information about **Heinemann Library** books.

To order:
☎ Phone 44 (0) 1865 888066
🗎 Send a fax to 44 (0) 1865 314091
💻 Visit the Heinemann Bookshop at www.heinemann.co.uk to browse our catalogue and order online.

First published in Great Britain by Heinemann Library, Halley Court, Jordan Hill, Oxford OX2 8EJ, a division of Reed Educational and Professional Publishing Ltd.

Heinemann is a registered trademark of Reed Educational & Professional Publishing Limited.

Oxford Melbourne Auckland Johannesburg Blantyre Gaborone Ibadan Portsmouth NH (USA) Chicago

© Reed Educational and Professional Publishing Ltd 2000
The moral right of the proprietor has been asserted.

Designed by M2 Graphic Design
Printed in Hong Kong / China
Originated by Ambassador Litho Ltd.

04 03 02 01 00
10 9 8 7 6 5 4 3 2 1

ISBN 0431 097798

British Library Cataloguing in Publication Data
Sean Connolly
Alcohol – (Need to know) 1. Alcohol – Juvenile literature 2. Alcoholism – Juvenile literature
I Title 362.2'98

Acknowledgements
The Publishers would like to thank the following for permission to reproduce photographs: Allsport: pg.23, pg.34; Bubbles: pg.48; Gareth Boden: pg.5, pg.11, pg.13, pg.26, pg.51; Impact: pg.6, pg.20, Martin Black pg.17, Chris Moyse pg.31, Piers Cavendish pg.37; Mary Evans Picture Library: pg.18, pg.21; Network: pg.9, pg.39, Barry Lewis pg.16, Homer Sykes pg.46; Photofusion: pg.15, pg.27, pg.29, pg.33, pg.35, pg.44, John Phillips pg.10, Paul Baldesare pg.22, pg.32, Steve Eason pg.47; Rex Features: pg.7, pg.25, pg.40, pg.41, pg.43; Science Photo Library: pg.12.

Cover photograph reproduced with permission of Tony Stone.

Any words appearing in the text in bold, **like this**, are explained in the Glossary.

Contents

Introduction 4

What is alcohol? 6

Taking effect 10

Addiction to alcohol 12

Alcohol in society 16

A long history 18

Who drinks alcohol? 22

A day in the life of a drinker 24

Exposure to alcohol 26

Easy availability 30

Groups at risk 32

The alcohol industry 34

The 'other' alcohol industry 38

Legal matters 40

Affecting a life 42

An ex-drinker's story 44

Treatment and counselling 46

People to talk to 50

Information and advice 52

Glossary 54

Index 56

Introduction

Alcohol is the most widely used drug in most western countries. It is part of the social scene, and its consumption goes virtually unnoticed at nearly every type of social gathering – from weddings and birthday parties to victory celebrations and even in religious ceremonies and funerals. For many people, taking the first alcoholic drink signifies the start of adulthood: young people are tempted to experiment with it and even to begin drinking regularly.

A powerful drug

Alcohol is a powerful drug, based on a chemical which can affect the brain's activities within minutes and produce lasting effects. These changes to the brain seem pleasurable in moderate amounts, because they build on feelings of confidence and relaxation. It is a fine line, however, between this 'feel good' state and one of **intoxication**, where a drinker's judgement and physical co-ordination become seriously disturbed.

In the same way, it is hard to distinguish between regular drinking in what seems to be moderate amounts – after work,

before watching a football match or at dinner – with what can gradually become a **dependence** on alcohol. Such dependence, often known loosely as **alcoholism**, is a serious problem for the drinker and for their family.

A happy balance

Some societies ban the use of alcohol for religious or other moral reasons. Others impose heavy taxes or other restrictions on its sale and use. These actions are a response to the known negative side-effects of alcohol. However, most readers of this book probably live in an area where alcohol is freely available to those old enough to buy it. Few obstacles lie in the way of getting 'hammered', 'wasted', 'trashed' or any of the many other words we have for being drunk. This freedom also reveals a full picture of the effects of the drug, how it can destroy lives if taken to excess, and how it can add to everyday enjoyment if taken in moderation.

After reading this book, you will be able to form your own decisions about alcohol and make responsible decisions for yourself.

What is alcohol?

Alcohol is a drug that affects people's behaviour in the short term and can have lasting effects if drunk in large quantities over a long period of time. Most people consume alcohol in a wide variety of alcoholic drinks, which are made up mainly of flavoured water and ethyl alcohol (**ethanol**). It is the ethanol that affects the brain, and the concentration of ethanol in a drink determines how **potent** it is. Most beers, lagers and ciders, for example, are made up of about one part ethanol to twenty parts of water. Stronger drinks contain correspondingly higher concentrations of ethanol: compared to beers and cider, wines contain about two to three times the amount of ethanol and spirits such as whisky and vodka have about ten times as much (being roughly half ethanol and half water).

The process of distillation is often very large scale, but it requires great care to ensure a consistent result.

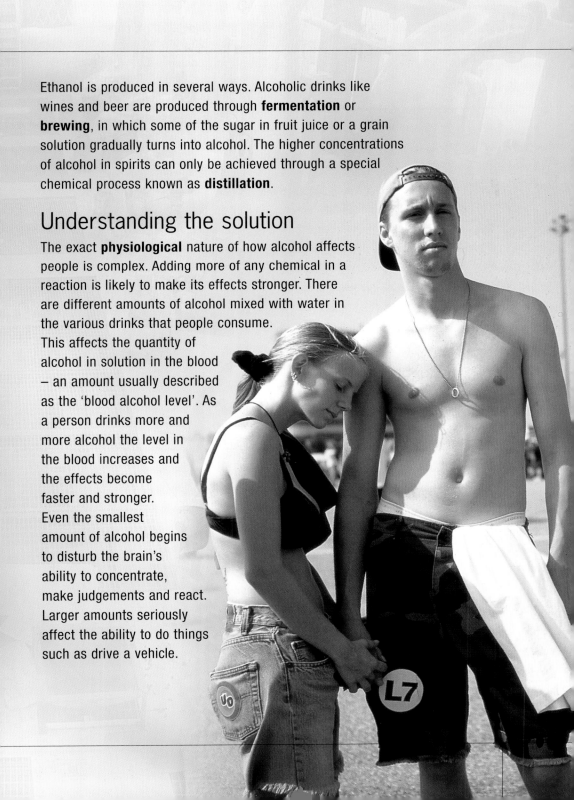

Ethanol is produced in several ways. Alcoholic drinks like wines and beer are produced through **fermentation** or **brewing**, in which some of the sugar in fruit juice or a grain solution gradually turns into alcohol. The higher concentrations of alcohol in spirits can only be achieved through a special chemical process known as **distillation**.

Understanding the solution

The exact **physiological** nature of how alcohol affects people is complex. Adding more of any chemical in a reaction is likely to make its effects stronger. There are different amounts of alcohol mixed with water in the various drinks that people consume. This affects the quantity of alcohol in solution in the blood – an amount usually described as the 'blood alcohol level'. As a person drinks more and more alcohol the level in the blood increases and the effects become faster and stronger. Even the smallest amount of alcohol begins to disturb the brain's ability to concentrate, make judgements and react. Larger amounts seriously affect the ability to do things such as drive a vehicle.

What is alcohol?

Other factors – also related to this chemical process – play a part in deciding how much or how quickly someone will be affected by alcohol. For example, women are usually affected more quickly because their bodies are smaller and contain less water. If there is less water to dilute the same amount of alcohol, the concentration of alcohol will be higher. Sometimes people say that a very muscular or obese person can 'really hold their drink' because the alcohol seems to have less effect on them. In fact, the body's extra muscle or fatty tissue absorbs some of the alcohol – leading to a lower concentration in the blood.

Consuming alcohol

People drink alcoholic beverages in a wide variety of situations – usually in a social setting. Alcohol's ability to 'loosen the tongue' is seen as an advantage at a party, for instance, where people might otherwise feel too shy to talk very much. Losing **inhibitions** in this way might also make people more willing to take chances or try things that usually worry them, for example an actor might take a drink before a performance to overcome stage fright. Bolstering confidence in this way is referred to as using 'Dutch courage'.
Some moderate use of alcohol is pardoned – or even expected – in many societies' but there is a fine balance between using alcohol to help people relax socially and letting it become a danger. The loss of co-ordination which occurs after several drinks – coupled with the false confidence produced by alcohol – can have terrible consequences, and many fatal accidents and crimes are linked with excessive drinking. In Britain alone, every year about 15,000 people are injured and 500 killed as a result of people drinking and driving.

Taking effect

The alcohol from a drink is absorbed very quickly into the bloodstream through the small intestine. Once in the bloodstream, the alcohol follows the same course as the blood itself. Since a great deal of blood is pumped continuously through the head, the alcohol soon finds its way to the area of the body where it has its most immediate effect. It can reach the brain as soon as five minutes after it is drunk. Fatty material in the brain absorbs alcohol effectively and the alcohol soon begins to take effect. The short-term effects are familiar to most people. Alcohol is a **depressant** drug and yet it reduces some social worries and allows people to relax.

The wide variety of alcoholic beverages caters for a wide range of tastes among the public.

After a couple of drinks the person becomes more relaxed and often more talkative. With more alcohol, however, the drinker begins to slur their words and becomes less co-ordinated. This process increases as more and more alcohol is consumed, until the drinker begins to stagger, 'see double' and feel sick. Many people pass out at this point, although larger doses can lead to serious complications such as unconsciousness, blindness, poisoning and even death.

Knowing the units

Health experts measure the amount of alcohol that people drink in units. This measurement provides the basis for general advice on the amounts of alcohol that can be drunk in reasonable safety. The following drinks contain a single unit of alcohol:

- one single pub measure (25 ml) of spirits
- one small glass (125 ml) of wine
- a half pint (255 ml) of ordinary strength (3.6 per cent alcohol) beer, lager or cider

The experts recommend upper drinking limits of 21 units a week for men and 14 units for women. These amounts should be spread out. Consistently drinking three or more units a day can cause harm.

Addiction to alcohol

Most people are familiar with the term 'alcoholic', although there is a great deal of ignorance surrounding both the term and our understanding of it. The word is often used jokingly about someone who has had one drink too many, or who is the one who suggests going out for a drink in the first place. Unfortunately, **alcoholism** is no laughing matter; it is a disease that affects many people and it has painful consequences for their friends and families. The problems range from financial and employment worries, through violence, divorce and a range of serious health concerns. Prolonged and excessive use can lead both directly and indirectly to death.

A problem of tolerance?

The problem of alcoholism is not so much to do with society's acceptance of drinking but with a drinker's physical **tolerance** to the effects of alcohol. Put simply, after a period of continued regular drinking, the same amount of alcohol produces a lesser effect than it did at first. The drinker consumes more alcohol to achieve the same effect as before.

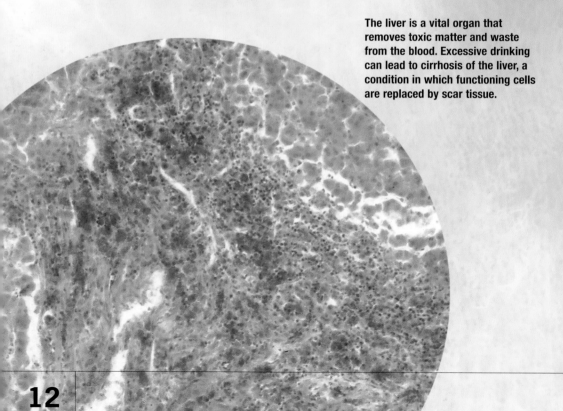

The liver is a vital organ that removes toxic matter and waste from the blood. Excessive drinking can lead to cirrhosis of the liver, a condition in which functioning cells are replaced by scar tissue.

The brain becomes affected as the amount of alcohol consumed increases, as the drinker seeks the same 'buzz'. A gradual sense of **dependence** builds up in the drinker, bringing with it a physical and psychological need for alcohol.

One of the dangers of alcohol is that such changes are not always obvious. Someone whose tolerance has built up may not seem drunk, even after consuming a large amount of alcohol. They might still seem able to work properly and generally appear in control. However, although the alcoholic effects on the brain that produce a 'high' have been lessened, the effects that are **toxic** to the brain cells themselves increase in line with the greater amounts being drunk. Sometimes the effects of these changes will only become obvious when the person develops a serious health problem, such as **cirrhosis** of the liver. Other people only become aware of a physical dependence when they suddenly find they are unable to drink for some reason. Such a sudden stoppage can lead to **withdrawal** symptoms such as jumpiness, sleeplessness, poor appetite, tremors ('the shakes') and even **hallucinations**.

Addiction to alcohol

Psychological effects

Physical **dependence** on alcohol is not the only problem. Heavy drinkers can develop psychological dependence, which affects the mind. The brain reacts to the stimulation of alcohol and starts to need it. The drinker craves alcohol for its psychological effects, such as relief from anxiety or extra confidence. A form of psychological dependence can develop even in someone who has not developed symptoms of physical dependence. The psychological dependence can be linked to drinking at certain times or on certain occasions – for example, before going to a party or a sporting event. Without access to alcohol, they may become anxious and suffer from panic attacks.

A family problem

A person's addiction to alcohol sends a shock wave through the rest of the family. Apart from concerns about the drinker's own health and other problems related to the drinking – such as drunk driving, violence and lack of judgement – the family lives in a state of tension. Heavy drinkers run the risk of losing their jobs and the very cost of drinking itself drains family resources.

Inherited risk

The family is also the focal point of another serious concern. There is considerable evidence that alcoholism runs in families. It now seems clear that the basis of alcohol dependence is partly **genetic**. It has been estimated that close relatives of alcoholics – such as children, siblings and parents – have a seven times greater chance of developing alcoholism than other people. It is not inevitable that they will become alcohol-dependent, but knowing the risk they can monitor their own drinking with greater seriousness.

An important distinction

Most people involved with alcohol **rehabilitation** make a distinction between alcohol abuse and alcohol dependence. Alcohol abuse, like the related terms 'drug abuse' and 'substance abuse', refers to a pattern of drinking that leads to health problems and personal problems. Dependence refers to the abnormal craving for alcohol – physical and psychological – that causes people to drink even when they know that their drinking is becoming a serious problem. It is this alcohol dependence that is often called alcoholism.

"I suppose I should have realized I had a problem when it was my turn to go up to the bar and order a large round of drinks for our table. I'd order an extra pint for myself and drink it before I returned with the drinks to my friends. Otherwise, my single pint would be long gone before the others had got halfway through theirs."

(Steve, an office worker who no longer drinks alcohol)

Alcohol in society

In most societies around the world, and in Western cultures in particular, alcohol is the 'drug of choice'. Apart from restrictions on age and in connection with driving there are few limits on its use. There are many reasons for this widespread use. The most understandable relate to the social functions of alcohol. There is a commonly held view that alcohol makes the good times better and helps people through the bad times.

People use alcohol to celebrate success, to soften the blows of sadness and defeat, and to mark special occasions such as weddings or the achievement of a university degree. In many religious denominations – for example Judaism and most Christian denominations – alcohol has a symbolic role and is used in services.

Everyday life

While many households have a drinks cupboard, a wine rack or several cans of lager in the refrigerator – for personal use in the home – the thing that sets alcohol apart from most other drugs is its social role. People enjoy drinking in groups and society caters for that fact. In the UK, for example, there are more than 80,000 pubs and bars that are designed for people drinking alcohol. In addition, there are more than 50,000 **off-licences** and 60,000 restaurants and clubs which sell alcohol.

Advertising, which emphasizes the 'good time' nature of alcohol, plays a part in keeping the numbers high – and rising. Advertising, and with it the sense that drinking alcohol is a 'grown-up' activity, means that young people drink more than older people. Other images, such as FA Cup winners or Formula 1 racing drivers showering themselves with champagne, send out signals that alcohol is linked with success. Boredom and a sense of danger also play a part in attracting young people to alcohol. As a result, drinkers in their late teens and early twenties consume 40–50 per cent more than the national average.

Underage drinking

In the UK it is illegal to sell alcohol to anyone under the age of 18. Nevertheless, underage drinking is widespread. A recent British study indicated that 60 per cent of 13–17-year-olds had bought alcohol in a pub or an off-licence. In the 13–16 age group about 30 per cent drink alcohol at least once a week.

A long history

Roman historians wrote about feasts and banquets where people would continue drinking wine until they became sick or passed out.

Alcoholic beverages date back many thousands of years and are mentioned in the written records of the earliest civilizations. Grapes grow in the wild in what we now call the Middle East, and people there noticed how grape juice would **ferment** to become wine.

Archaeologists have suggested that the first cultivated **vineyards** were developed in the Caucasus region (near present-day Georgia and Armenia) between 6000 and 4000BC.

The technique of grape cultivation and fermentation, as well as of **brewing** beer, spread throughout the Middle East and became firmly established in the societies of ancient Mesopotamia and Egypt.

Setting the pattern

The ancient Greeks began what might be called the 'alcohol industry' by fermenting their wines in resin-coated vats and then filtering the wines into clay storage vessels for export. The Romans followed the Greek example, planting vineyards across their empire wherever the soil and climate were favourable.

The fall of the Roman Empire in the fifth century AD spelt the end, temporarily, of widespread cultivation of vineyards. Europeans still produced wine, but the quality had declined and most of it was used for religious purposes. Beers and ales remained popular, as well as other drinks such as mead (made from fermented honey).

The biggest development was the discovery of **distillation**. This process concentrates the amount of alcohol in a liquid while removing many of the unpleasant-tasting impurities. Distilling had long been practised in east Asia but it was Arabs who brought it to prominence in the Middle East and Europe. The first recorded mention of distillation was made by Abul Kasim, a tenth-century Arab doctor. By the following century Europeans had learnt the technique and the Irish, soon followed by the Scots, distilled grains to produce the first whiskies.

As the Middle Ages gave way to the **Renaissance**, the seeds of present-day drinking patterns in Europe had been sown. Good-quality wine was once more available from southern countries, while northern Europeans had mastered the art of producing beers and ales. Eastern Europeans distilled and drank vodka. Pubs, beer cellars, taverns and wayside inns sold these drinks, which were now woven into the social fabric of most nations.

Stronger and cheaper

A great change occurred in the eighteenth century, when gin was introduced to Britain. Gin is a spirit, like whisky or vodka, but at that time it was far easier and cheaper to produce and it required no ageing before it could be drunk. As a result supplies of gin seemed to flood the market in British cities, and the level of drunkenness soared. It was said that with gin one could get 'drunk for a penny, dead drunk for tuppence'.

By the beginning of the nineteenth century Britain had enacted some laws to control widespread drinking. The Gin Act, passed in the eighteenth century, had raised the cost of the drink. Laws in the nineteenth century aimed to ban young people from pubs. Leading the campaign against alcohol were religious leaders and an anti-alcohol group called the **Temperance Movement**, which was also active in the United States.

Modern approaches

The modern system of **licensing** and opening hours was developed in Britain during the **First World War** because of concerns about the effects alcohol was having on soldiers and workers in ammunition factories. Soon after the war ended, the United States took even more drastic action to control alcohol. In 1919 it banned alcoholic drinks altogether. This ban, called the **Prohibition**, lasted until 1933. However, the public was not happy with this ban and many people either smuggled in alcohol from other countries or tried to make their own.

The American experiment with Prohibition showed how difficult it was for a government to stop people drinking if society already tolerated alcohol. Political leaders still frown on excessive drinking but the modern approach to the problem is to mount public-awareness campaigns. Nowadays, people can buy drinks in a theme pub, a wine bar, various types of restaurant and café and even in the supermarket. With this choice, however, comes the expectation that the adult population will be aware of what constitutes sensible drinking, and what poses a problem for themselves and for others.

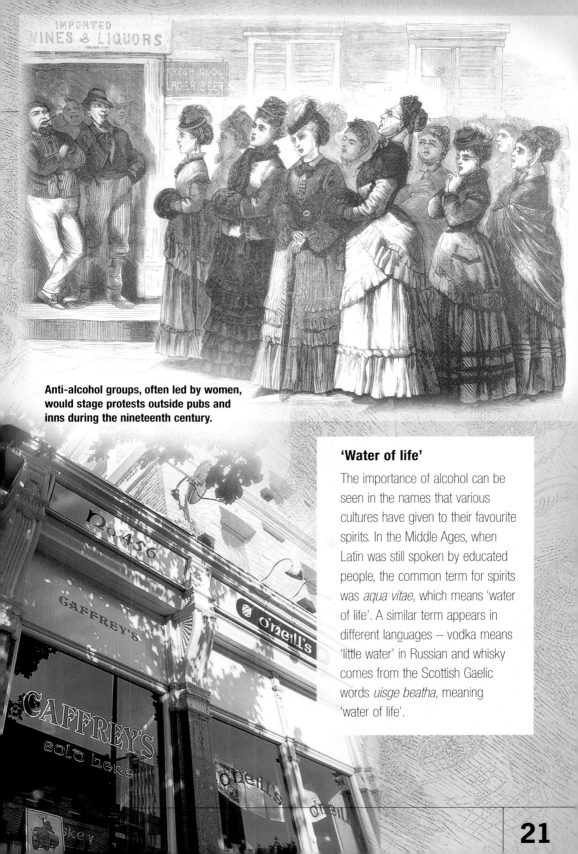

Anti-alcohol groups, often led by women, would stage protests outside pubs and inns during the nineteenth century.

'Water of life'

The importance of alcohol can be seen in the names that various cultures have given to their favourite spirits. In the Middle Ages, when Latin was still spoken by educated people, the common term for spirits was *aqua vitae*, which means 'water of life'. A similar term appears in different languages – vodka means 'little water' in Russian and whisky comes from the Scottish Gaelic words *uisge beatha*, meaning 'water of life'.

Who drinks alcohol?

In many countries – in particular those where most of the population is Muslim – consumption of alcoholic drinks is either prohibited or severely restricted. Religious objections have also traditionally led to local restrictions on its sale in parts of Scandinavia, Wales and Scotland. In such areas, being even mildly drunk would be seen as an insult to the local population.

Elsewhere, however, alcohol is part of the way of life for many people. For example, more than 90 per cent of the adult British population drinks alcohol regularly. On average, men drink the equivalent of 1.5 pints of beer a day and women 0.5 pints. One in five men drinks the equivalent of around three to four pints or more at least once a week.

A young person's problem

Most of the adult drinking occurs at social occasions that society feels are appropriate for alcohol – at parties, with a group in a pub, dining out or at special occasions such as weddings. Britain's more liberal **licensing** laws, allowing Sunday opening and more venues serving alcohol, have made drinking a more relaxed affair than it was. In the past it was common for men to go out to the pub, leaving the rest of the family at home while they drank pint after pint.

Nowadays couples and families tend to be part of the drinking picture. Young people are often present and can be exposed to alcohol in limited amounts.

Without guidance, however, young people are inclined to drink more than their adult counterparts. They tend to get drunk more often, drink more in one session and to drink stronger beers, lagers and ciders. In addition, they have been the target of advertisers marketing extra strong lagers and ciders in recent years. These new products have been followed by the controversial '**alcopops**', which look and taste like soft drinks but have a higher alcoholic content than many beers.

Early decisions

The drinking habits that young people develop can often remain with them for life. Repeated excessive drinking can pave the way for 'problem drinking' and **alcoholism** in later years. A sensible approach, adopted early on, however, usually allows a person to maintain moderate drinking patterns throughout their life. There is another important reason for avoiding excessive drinking: young people need to have their brains functioning clearly to meet the intellectual demands of learning and preparation for a career.

The leading drivers traditionally douse each other with champagne at the end of a Formula One motor race.

A day in the life of a drinker

Since most adults drink some alcohol regularly – and usually with no lasting ill effects or **dependence** – it would be misleading to focus on just one person. However, the picture becomes different, and recurring themes begin to emerge, when we talk about someone who drinks excessively. Differences in social background, income, musical tastes and even personality diminish as alcohol begins to assume increasing importance in their lives.

The morning after

For most heavy drinkers, the day begins with a **hangover**. Sudden movements, sharp noises and even eating are enough to make the upset stomach and headache feel even worse. There is a strong temptation to stay in bed and sleep it off, calling in sick for work or missing classes at college. Very heavy drinkers try to overcome the feeling by taking another alcoholic drink – the 'hair of the dog' – often leading to a very early start to the day's drinking.

Daytime sessions

The hours crawl by to lunchtime, when the drinker usually heads off to a pub or bar. The typical heavy drinker will be one of the first to arrive and almost always one of the last to leave. During this time an excessive drinker will have three or more pints – or the equivalent – before returning to an unproductive afternoon.

An evening spent at a film, play or sporting event is not an attractive choice for a heavy drinker, since it guarantees several hours of 'non-drinking time'. This idea is partly accepted by society: for example, slogans on T-shirts often joke about the importance of maximizing drinking time. The reality for someone who is dependent on alcohol is different. The need to drink is like a craving. Even social occasions, where alcohol is a feature, become excuses for heavy drinking.

During the course of the evening the quantities consumed over lunchtime are doubled or more, conversations become blurred and other people's feelings mean little. Bedtime is rarely a chance to reflect calmly on the day's events. The heavy drinker will often crash out on a sofa and need to be helped to bed by a friend or family member. Sleep is hardly refreshing. If the drinker is conscious before going to bed, they will know that the cycle is likely to be repeated the next day.

Sobering facts

- One in 25 people in Britain is dependent on alcohol.
- 1.4 million men (six per cent of the overall adult male population) and 500,000 women (two per cent of the overall female population) are drinking at very risky levels, over 50 units a week for men and 35 units for women.

Exposure to alcohol

Alcohol is widely available in most countries and has become central to the fabric of many societies. The ways in which alcohol – and its abuse – have filtered into everyday life are varied and subtle. The occasional 'tipsy' lapse is excused, the comic drunk is a mainstay of the entertainment business, and many students and young sports fans view alcohol as a gateway to adulthood.

Freedom of choice

Many societies have moved on from the days when it was felt that people's personal lives could be dictated by government. Most national experiments to stamp out drinking, such as the US **Prohibition**, have failed. Modern life revolves instead around personal choice and individual responsibility. So governments warn the public about the dangers of alcohol through product labelling and public-service advertising campaigns.

This freedom of choice also means that the alcohol industry is also free to influence people's behaviour. A stylish magazine advertisement or a commercial on cinema or television screens might portray alcohol as an essential element for a brash party or a tropical paradise.

Home-brew kits offer people an inexpensive way to produce beer or wine at home. However; without proper supervision, they can be a recipe for excessive drinking – sending out the wrong signal to young family members.

Advertisers know just how far broadcasting restrictions will allow them to go in implying that alcohol is a necessary part of these good times. In some countries, such as the United States, they will even have to include some wording about the dangers of alcohol. The gullible, who include many impressionable young people, will ignore this sobering postscript and remember only the good times promised on the ski slopes, in a Mississippi paddle boat or surfing on the Australian coast.

Market awareness

Most teenagers are aware which drinks provide a powerful kick, which taste sweet and are easy to drink, and which are the cheapest. Young people are now very well informed about the whole range of drinks, even if they find the medical warnings easy to ignore. Alcoholic drinks are on sale everywhere, from the traditional spots such as pubs and **off-licences** to supermarkets, cafés and snack bars. Despite specific laws about underage drinking, the statistics indicate that young people are able to get hold of alcohol.

Peer pressure plays a part in many young people's introduction to alcohol. The example of friends who obtain alcohol – often while still too young to drink legally – is a powerful incentive to follow suit. Being the odd one out, in this case the one who refuses to get drunk with their friends, can expose young people to ridicule.

The role of the family

Because alcohol is so widespread and deeply rooted in western society, many people have lost track of an important fact: alcohol is a drug. Some parents are deeply concerned about the risks their children face from exposure to cocaine, ecstasy and **hallucinogenic** drugs. Many of these adults concentrate so hard on these drugs that they ignore or even accept patterns of regular heavy drinking from their children. In such instances, the parents are missing out on an important responsibility – to provide sound advice and an example about sensible drinking.

Many families, however, recognize the need to introduce young people to the whole concept of sensible drinking, showing by example and inclusion how moderate use of alcohol is a better idea – and more enjoyable – than **binge drinking** to excess. Again, this more positive approach can be explained in part by the modern 'freedom of choice'. Families out for a Sunday ramble in the countryside can now feel happier about stopping for a pub lunch. Instead of being met by unwelcoming managers and crowds of heavy drinkers in a smoky interior, families can now enjoy a meal – and the parents can still drink – in comfortable dining rooms or in outside areas. The alcohol is no barrier to the group's enjoyment of the day, and children can appreciate how moderate drinking forms part of the overall sense of relaxation.

Foreign examples

Experiences gained from travelling can also help build good images of drinking. In many countries in continental Europe – such as France, Spain and Italy – wine is present at most family gatherings, from simple picnics to special celebrations. Some of the children are even encouraged to take a few sips from their parents' glasses. In such a setting, even young children learn that alcohol is not **taboo**, but that there are accepted limits to how much people should drink. This is not to ignore the fact that these same countries still deal with problems of **alcoholism** and problem drinking. However, in general, it is expected that drinkers will behave sensibly, and public drunkenness – including that of young people – is not seen as 'part of growing up'.

"My parents don't mind if I drink; they like it better than drugs, anyway."

(Teenager quoted in J. Haskins, *Teenage Alcoholism*, Hawthorn Books, 1976)

Easy availability

Alcohol is easily available across most of the western world, despite some regulations and limitations on the hours during which it can be sold, age limits and other restraining factors. The prices of alcoholic drinks vary widely, ranging from less than a pound for a large bottle of strong British cider and several dollars for a large bottle of wine in the United States to bottles of some **vintage** wines that cost as much as a car.

The role of the government

One reason why banning alcohol is unpopular – quite apart from issues about limiting personal freedoms – is that alcoholic drinks supply large amounts of money to most governments. In Britain, for example, the cost of a bottle of spirits includes more than £5 tax which goes to the government. A bottle of wine includes a tax of more than a pound and every pint of beer includes more than 25 pence tax.

In the UK, it is the Chancellor of the Exchequer who decides on the amount of tax to be paid on alcohol. This is stated in the annual Budget Speech. In addition to raising money, Budget taxes can be used to try to persuade people to use less of a product because of the increased price. This idea partly underlies the taxes on alcohol and, more particularly, the taxes added to the price of tobacco and petrol.

Popular demand

Despite these annual increases in the cost of alcohol – government taxes on drink are rarely lowered – there is intense competition among establishments selling alcohol. Supermarkets and wine warehouses compete with **off-licences**, and many people return from foreign holidays with large amounts of drinks bought at **duty-free** shops, which do not charge the extra national taxes. In addition, Europeans are free to return from other European countries with as much alcohol as they want – for their personal use – and these drinks often cost less on the Continent than in Britain. Such a thriving business in discount alcohol makes it easier for young people to afford a variety of drinks, even if they can no longer expect to get 'drunk for a penny, dead drunk for tuppence'. Lower costs of alcohol, with a wide range of settings in which to drink it, can offer a good introduction to sensible drinking. They can also make it easy to develop problems with alcohol.

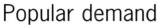

Groups at risk

While excessive drinking and **dependence** on alcohol are problems for society in general, certain sections of the population face particular risks with alcohol. Young people, with their tendency to drink more than average, are at the forefront. The risks from underage drinking, which include violence, serious injuries and accidental death, are well documented. **Binge drinking** is common in this age group, leading to immediate physical side-effects and increased **tolerance** to alcohol.

Early damage

Research into the effects of alcohol on the brain are still at an early stage. Scientists know that the brain does not finish developing until a person is about twenty years old, and the area responsible for making complex judgements is one of the last to mature. Repeated bouts of heavy drinking, with the risk of dependence on alcohol, is likely to cause irreparable damage to the cells in this part of the brain.

Years ago, the taste of beer or spirits – not naturally attractive for young people who were used to sweetened soft drinks – tended to slow down consumption of alcohol among the young. Newer products, in particular **alcopops**, have been attracting young people because they taste much more like the familiar childhood drinks. It is very easy to consume excessive amounts of these sweetened alcoholic drinks, and thereby sow the seeds for later problems of alcohol dependence.

Young men face another specific problem. In studies comparing the sons of alcoholic fathers with those of non-alcoholic fathers, it seems that the first group experiences the pleasant effects of alcohol more strongly – and the damaging effects less strongly – than the second. With the negative side-effects less likely to act as a brake on heavy drinking, these young men face more risk of becoming addicted, like their fathers.

Risks for women

Women of any age experience different effects from alcohol than those felt by men. Being on average smaller than men, they feel the effects of a given amount of alcohol more acutely. They also experience greater physical damage to the liver and pancreas with comparatively smaller amounts of alcohol, while also running a greater risk of developing high blood pressure.

Sobering facts

- Up to 40 per cent of child abuse cases are alcohol-related.
- Eighteen to twenty-four year olds have the highest consumption of alcohol at unsafe levels.
- Even small amounts of alcohol drunk by pregnant women can lead to babies with low birth-weights.
- Men drinking more than the equivalent of three pints of beer a day risk low sperm counts and even **infertility**.

33

The alcohol industry

It comes as no surprise to learn that alcohol is big business. It generates vast amounts of money in the form of profits (for producers of alcoholic beverages as well as for distributors and outlets selling alcohol) and in tax revenues for governments. Even though overall consumption of alcohol is no longer increasing rapidly – and there have been some recent years when it actually declined somewhat – the industry has become far more sophisticated. In many ways, so has the general public.

Capturing trends

It is hard to say how much the drinks industry follows social trends in drinking – and how much it leads them through advertising and marketing. Sales of wine are a good example of this mixed picture. In the years following the **Second World War**, and right through most of the 1960s, wine was very much a minority drink in Britain and the United States. The well-off drank it with dinner and other people tended to have it mainly at special occasions such as weddings.

Large brewers have long associated themselves with major competitions in sports, such as football.

The change in this pattern came in the 1970s, as average incomes rose (making wine seem more affordable) and people began taking more holidays abroad, where they were more exposed to wine. Even then, however, it was uncommon to see wine on the shelves of supermarkets.

Now wine is a mainstream drink in most western countries, with wine columns in newspapers informing readers about the best **vintages**, good bargains and how to store expensive bottles. The choice of wines is enormous, as are the variations in how it is sold. People can buy wine by the individual bottle, the twelve-bottle case, the half-bottle, or even in wine boxes from which the contents can be poured through a built-in tap.

Niche marketing

Wine is not the only alcoholic drink to be produced in far greater variety than in bygone years. The alcohol industry, like others involved in sales, understands that different segments of the population prefer different types of drinks. Selling a range of similar products, with a few small variations, is called 'niche marketing'. It is now common. Buyers can also choose among vodkas made from different grains and flavouring, rums of various darknesses and strengths, pre-mixed cocktails, and low-alcohol variations of familiar drinks. Beers, which make up nearly two-thirds of alcohol sales in the United States and elsewhere, come in bewildering varieties, including light beers, ice beers, lagers, real ales, Pilsners and low-alcohol and non-alcoholic tipples. **Microbreweries** have been set up to supply beers only to local pubs and bars.

It is this strategy of niche marketing that has led drinks producers to target the younger market. **Alcopops** are the most obvious example of this trend, and few people over the age of twenty would be interested in them. Extra-strength beers and ciders, although supposedly aimed at the general public, are advertised heavily with films that attract young audiences.

Responsible marketing?

Despite being able to generate huge profits through sales, the alcohol industry must also adjust to a changing climate. The general public is now more informed about the dangers of alcohol, the risks associated with young people drinking and with drink-driving offences. There has been a strong and well-organized public reaction against the introduction of **alcopops** in the UK and Australia – from parents, teachers and drink-awareness groups. In response, alcohol companies have had to tone down the marketing of these drinks – and similar products in the United States – to extend their appeal beyond the youth market.

Drink-driving is an area of particular concern. Following the intense public reaction to the rise in deaths and injuries stemming from drunk drivers, the alcohol industry has been trying to dissuade people from driving after having anything to drink. In the 1970s the Seagrams Corporation, a major Canadian **distiller**, introduced a scheme to pay for the travelling costs of New Year's party-goers on public transport in Montreal. In the United States, many bars and clubs operate a 'designated driver' scheme. One person in a group, who will drive the others home, agrees not to drink during an entire evening. The driver receives a badge to wear and gets free soft drinks and sometimes big discounts on food as well.

❝We do not target our advertising at young people. Period.❞

(Stephen Lambright, Vice President, Anheuser-Busch – makers of Budweiser)

Pressure groups

It is common in western countries for people to form groups in order to influence elected officials in Parliament, the US Congress and other law-making bodies. Such associations are called **pressure groups**. Companies involved with alcohol production try to influence law-makers by arguing for fewer restrictions on distribution, lower taxes on alcohol and in other areas. Arguing the opposite case – for more control over the distribution and sale of alcohol – are groups such as Alcohol Concern in the UK and MADD (Mothers Against Drunk Driving) in the United States.

It is claimed that alcopops aim to lure young drinkers with their brightly coloured labels and the sweet taste of the drinks themselves.

The 'other' alcohol industry

Our widespread thirst for alcohol has led to a boom in another industry – the medical profession. Although hardly welcomed by doctors, nurses and other health-care workers, alcohol provides extra work for doctors' surgeries, hospital wards and intensive-care units. Some of the causes are obviously related to alcohol, such as alcohol poisoning from drinking too much, and the terrible numbers of injuries and deaths arising from drink-driving accidents.

What is less well known is that alcohol underpins a whole range of other injuries and crimes, which at first glance seem unrelated to drink. In the UK alcohol has been estimated to be a factor in:

- 30 per cent of drownings
- 33 per cent of accidents at home
- 45 per cent of woundings and assaults
- at least 39 per cent of deaths in fires.

Similar statistics apply in the United States, where one person dies every 30 minutes in an alcohol-related road accident.

The medical cost of alcohol

All of this costs money – huge amounts of it. The National Health Service (NHS) in Britain spends more than £160 million each year on treating alcohol-related illness. In the United States it has been estimated that twenty per cent of hospital costs and eight per cent of overall health-care costs are alcohol-related. These costs, arising either indirectly through accidents or directly through the use of alcohol, could be dramatically reduced if people were more aware of the dangers of alcohol.

There are further effects on the economy, even if they are comparatively hidden. In Britain, industry in general loses £2 billion every year through lost **productivity**, unemployment and absenteeism due to workers drinking alcohol.

Sobering facts

- Some 25,000–28,000 people die each year in Britain from alcohol-related illnesses: this is 50 times the annual rate of deaths from all illicit drugs put together.
- Approximately one dollar of social costs is created for every retail dollar spent on alcoholic beverages in the United States.

Young revellers are out for a good time but their antics can be dangerous and pose a threat to public safety.

Legal matters

In Britain, the 1964 **Licensing** Act controls most of the manufacture, sale, distribution and purchase of alcohol. Under this Act venues such as pubs and clubs are granted 'on-licences', meaning that people can buy and drink alcohol on the premises. Retail establishments known as **off-licences** are granted 'off-licences' which allow them to sell alcohol that can be taken away to be consumed off the premises. Special licenses also apply to restaurants and some forms of transport such as trains. Other laws, some of them enacted locally, specify where people can drink in public.

'Over the limit'

The most serious connection between alcohol and the law relates to the issue of drink-driving. Usually, a driver suspected of being drunk is pulled over after speeding, driving recklessly (or even over-carefully) or being involved in an accident. The driver is asked to blow into a device known as a **breathalyser**. This has red, yellow and green lights to indicate how much alcohol a driver has consumed.

The UK, in common with nearly every other country, has strict laws about how much alcohol a driver can consume before driving. A driver is over the limit if there are more than 80 mg of alcohol in every 100 ml of blood. This ratio is also expressed as a .08 **BAC** (blood alcohol content) level.

BAC to basics

The UK level of .08 BAC is the same as that in several other western countries, including Austria, Canada and Switzerland. **Pressure groups** concerned about alcohol abuse and road safety press for this figure to be lowered. Germany did just that, on 1 May 1998, when it lowered the BAC from .08 to .05 – the same figure as Australia. The results show that the move has been a great success. Compared with similar figures before the limit was lowered, there was a 13 per cent drop in accidents involving drink-driving. More encouragingly, there was a drop of nearly 12 per cent in deaths arising from drink-driving accidents. In the United States, where BAC levels are determined by each state, most states have a high level of .10.

In the UK it is against the law:

- to give alcohol to a child under five except under medical supervision
- for a young person under 14 (under 18 in Northern Ireland) to be in a bar, unless the licensee has a children's certificate
- for a licensee knowingly to sell alcohol to a person under 18, with the exception that young people over 16 can buy porter, cider or perry with a meal in a dining room in a public house or hotel and can consume beer bought by an accompanying person over 18.

In Australia:

- it is an offence to sell alcohol to people less than 18 years of age or to people who are intoxicated
- it is illegal to drive with a blood alcohol content over .05
- penalties for drunk driving offences include disqualification from driving for a set period, fines and imprisonment.

Affecting a life

Prolonged and heavy drinking of alcohol creates a range of serious side-effects, both for the drinker and for their family. It is a problem that crosses boundaries of gender, wealth and social status. The physical risks are well known, and a British **pharmaceutical** group has concluded that an individual who continues to drink heavily is likely to die about fifteen years earlier than the expected average. The main causes of premature death are heart disease, cancer, accidents and suicide. Tied in with this suicide figure is the problem of depression that arises among many heavy drinkers.

Why do they do it?

There are probably as many answers to this question as there are heavy drinkers. Although generalizations are often inaccurate, it can be said that people with great responsibility, or whose work involves long hours and little supervision, figure highly in the ranks of problem drinkers. This group often includes people who are in the public eye, such as actors, politicians and athletes.

Many of these high-profile drinkers have turned their fame to good advantage, using their own well-publicized struggles as guidelines for others facing the same problem. Betty Ford, the wife of former US President Gerald Ford, admitted to alcohol addiction in the 1970s. She has been instrumental in setting up the Betty Ford **Rehabilitation** Centers, which help others overcome their addictions to alcohol and drugs.

Sportsmen who 'go dry'

Despite the widespread assumption that top sportsmen – footballers in particular – should be able to 'hold their drink', a number of players have admitted to being addicted to alcohol and have taken steps to recover. Footballer Tony Adams, the Arsenal and England defender, admitted such a problem in 1996 and has since been a prominent spokesman in raising public awareness of the problem. Paul Merson, now with Aston Villa, had a similar experience in 1995. He broke down in tears in October 1998 as he compared the recent stories about Paul Gascoigne's alcohol problems with his own experiences with addiction. His advice about Gascoigne was simple: 'If he stops drinking and gets better, there's nobody in the England squad who can touch him – not even David Beckham'. It is that degree of hopefulness that helps addicts take control of their lives.

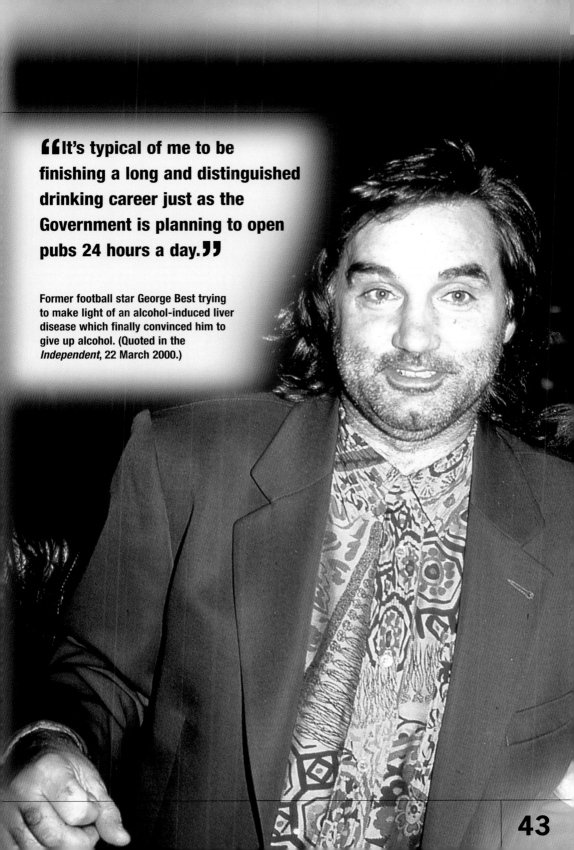

"It's typical of me to be finishing a long and distinguished drinking career just as the Government is planning to open pubs 24 hours a day."

Former football star George Best trying to make light of an alcohol-induced liver disease which finally convinced him to give up alcohol. (Quoted in the *Independent*, 22 March 2000.)

An ex-drinker's story

Philip (not his real name) is a journalist who went through a period of heavy drinking in his mid-twenties but found it was taking over his life.

"I was working on a news magazine where there was a real buzz – late-breaking news, scoops and all the sorts of excitement that I had hoped for when I became a journalist. We'd work late sometimes, in order to 'put the magazine to bed' (finish an issue before the deadline), so it also meant that daytime hours could be a little irregular."

The crunch

"I soon found that the pub was the best place to learn more about what was happening behind the scenes at work. Bit by bit, my drinking grew – from a pint or maybe two, to four or more pints in a session. I felt a bit embarrassed about this, so I used to make excuses about not joining the others and then I'd go off to another pub and drink on my own. Back at work after a session I sometimes became abusive, which was really out of character. My editor was sympathetic, but he told me that people were concerned about my drinking. Much as he liked me, I'd face warnings and possible dismissal if it continued.

That really shook me up. I told my wife about this meeting, and she suggested going to a psychological counsellor. The counsellor, who wasn't really a specialist in alcohol matters, was great. In fact, it turned out that the stress and the excitement of the job – which I had found stimulating at first – were getting me down. I was drinking to avoid confronting these and a few personal problems."

A test of willpower

"No one forced me to do anything, but I made a promise to my wife to stop drinking. It was also a test for myself, to see if I had the willpower. I found it really hard at first, but most of my friends encouraged me and accepted my not drinking without trying to persuade me back. I took another look at my life, found a job in a less stressful environment and began to feel like my old self. This happened a few years ago now, and although I might take the odd glass of wine, I never regret that decision to call it quits."

Treatment and counselling

Recent years have seen great advances in the treatment and care of people who are **dependent** on alcohol. As society has grasped the importance of addressing the problem – and increasingly considers **alcoholism** as a disease – new methods of treatment have been developed. Having several alternatives available means that each drinker can choose the setting or the approach that best suits their needs, but the first step must come from the drinker.

Admitting the need

People come to terms with their own drinking problems in a number of ways. The most dramatic, of course, are when they are faced with some immediate physical effect of alcohol, such as alcohol poisoning, or if they have failed a breath test while driving. Others might be told by friends or family members. Still others draw the conclusion without any outside influence. It is a hard problem to admit, especially since there is so much outside pressure to continue drinking.

Some problem drinkers feel accused and deny that there really is a problem. Alcohol-abuse counsellors can take some of the blame from drinkers by offering a **screening** test. Two of the most common of these tests use easily remembered abbreviations. One of them, known as the CAGE, asks the following questions.

- Have you ever felt the need to **C**ut down on your drinking?
- Have you ever felt **A**nnoyed by someone criticizing your drinking?
- Have you ever felt **G**uilty about your drinking?
- Have you ever felt the need for an **E**ye-opener (a drink at the beginning of the day)?

If a person answers 'yes' to two or more of these questions, there is a good chance that they have a problem with alcohol. The next step is for them to face up to the need to solve the problem, by getting information and setting about changing their drinking habits. The best first step in this process is cutting out drinking, even if the goal is not one of lifetime **abstinence**. This is a very hard decision to make, and many people need the support of others to help them through their period of transition. Knowing what facilities are available can help the person choose between coming to terms with their problem in a group – as with organizations such as Alcoholics Anonymous – or in a more personal one-to-one setting.

Treatment and counselling

Interview with a counsellor

Nick Corrigan is a youth counsellor with Advice and Counselling on Alcohol and Drugs (ACAD) in Bristol, England. He has noted an increase in the number of young people coming to ACAD for treatment, based largely on what he terms the 'widespread acceptability of drinking culture'. He is less concerned with widespread anxieties about **alcopops** – which he believes are less popular than people imagine – and more worried about the drinking patterns of young people. 'Younger drinkers are more inclined to **binge drink**, which is really a way to build up problems in later life. It's this message that we try to get across in workshops and seminars.

'The system of units, which works as a guideline for adults, doesn't really apply to young people, whose smaller and less developed bodies absorb alcohol more easily. There's also a problem with some ethnic minority communities, where alcohol is frowned upon or forbidden. Some families won't accept that there's even any drinking among the young, let alone problem drinking.'

Young people, some as young as eleven, come to ACAD with alcohol problems. The organization works with local schools and youth organizations to provide workshops, with question-and-answer sessions fielded by volunteers. 'Bristol is typical in its youth drinking problems, but the solution here, as elsewhere, lies in getting the full message across.'

Changing attitudes

Some people look at a homeless person, passed out by an empty bottle of cheap wine, and feel superior. Such a reaction, which suggests that the sleeping drinker somehow 'had it coming' by taking to drink, ignores the fact that **alcoholism** is a disease. True, it is brought on by personal choice – the decision to take the first drink – but it can gather momentum so that the choice to stop becomes harder and harder. A better understanding of this disease would make people realize that the person needs counselling and help, rather than a simple condemnation.

Sobering facts

- One in four acute male hospital admissions in Britain is alcohol-related.
- There were over 22,800 UK hospital admissions in one year (1994–5) due to alcohol **dependence** or the **toxic** effects of alcohol.

People to talk to

There are very few drugs that people begin to take on their own, for private recreation. More often, people get 'high' or 'buzzed' in the company of others. Young people are no exception, and neither is alcohol. While it is true that alcohol is drunk in a number of settings, including solitary drinking, it is usually the group that forms the basis of young people's drinking. Word of mouth – both about what it's like being drunk and how 'cool' it is meant to be – form the basis of many people's introduction to alcohol. This type of **peer pressure** is not helpful, but it is a strong and persuasive force.

Other voices

There are people who can put alcohol in a different perspective, either by giving first-hand accounts of their own drinking experiences or by outlining the clear dangers of alcohol. Parents and older family members are usually the best people to turn to first. However, the teenage years are often the period when young people feel that they have least in common with their parents. Even sympathetic teachers and others in authority locally might seem too close to home.

The UK has a wide range of telephone contacts – many of them free of charge and most of them anonymous – where young people can find out more about how alcohol is affecting them. Many of the organizations listed in the Information and advice section (pages 52–3) are specialist phone lines. They provide a confidential telephone service, or they can suggest local agencies throughout the UK. Others are geared specifically to queries coming from younger people. Whether you approach one of these organizations, or a family member, a youth leader or teacher, the important thing is to be able to talk – and listen – freely about alcohol concerns. Sharing a problem or worry is the first step to solving it.

Information and advice

There are many organizations in the field of alcohol and drug awareness that can provide detailed information or confidential advice about the use and abuse of alcohol. Most offer information over the phone, or provide information packs and leaflets dealing with alcohol abuse and how it affects individuals and their families. Many of these organizations are regionally based, and can act as a springboard for getting information about specific local agencies.

Alcohol Recovery Project (ARP), Central Office, 68 Newington Causeway, Southwark, London SE1 6DF Tel: 020 7403 3369 www.arp-charity.demon.co.uk
ARP covers the London area and offers information on other regional centres in the UK.

British National Temperance League (BNTL), Westbrook Court, 2 Sharrow Vale Road, Sheffield S11 8YZ, Tel/fax: 0114 267 9976
The BNTL, based on a Christian foundation, promotes healthy drug-free lifestyles and acts together with other organizations aimed at individuals and communities.

Campaign Against Drinking and Driving (CADD), 83 Jesmond Road, Newcastle Upon Tyne NE2 1NH Tel: 0191 281 1581
CADD supports the victims and families injured or killed by drunk and irresponsible drivers.

Health Education Board for Scotland (HEBS), Woodburn House, Canaan Lane, Edinburgh EH10 4SG Tel: 0131 536 5500 www.hebs.scot.nhs.uk
HEBS is responsible for health promotion and health education in Scotland.

Health Promotion Wales, Ffynnon-las, Ty Glas Avenue, Llanishen, Cardiff CF4 5DZ Tel: 029 2075 2222
Health Promotion Wales is responsible for health promotion and health education in Wales.

Hope UK, 25f Copperfield Street, London SE1 0EN Tel: 020 7928 0848
Hope UK educates young people on the problem that alcohol and other drugs cause.

Northern Ireland Community Addiction Service (NICA), 40 Elmwood Avenue, Belfast BT9 6AZ, Tel: 01232 664434
NICA offers advice and counselling to people with alcohol and drug problems and their families.

Specialist phone lines

Asianline, Tel: 0345 32 02 02, Monday
1pm–8pm (charged at local rates)
Tel: 0990 133 480 dial and listen available
in Hindi and Urdu (charged at local rates)
This National Alcohol Helpline for Asians is
entirely confidential and is currently available in
Hindi, Urdu, Gujarati and Punjabi.

Drinkline: National Alcohol Helpline
Tel: 0345 32 02 02 Helpline calls (charged
at local rates)
Tel: 0500 801 802 Freephone, dial and
listen service with recorded messages about
alcohol problems (24 hours)
Drinkline is for anyone who needs help or
information about alcohol. It provides help to
callers worried about their own drinking or that
of a family member. It also refers callers to
local Alcohol Advice Agencies.

Drinkline Youth, Tel: 0345 32 02 02
Helpline calls (charged at local rates)
Tel: 0990 143 275 dial and listen service,
24 hours (charged at local rate)
Drinkline Youth is a service provided by
Drinkline, and the helpline number
(11am–11pm Monday to Friday) is the same as
that of Drinkline, so make sure you ask for
Drinkline Youth. This service also provides a
range of information packs aimed specifically
at young people.

Further reading

Alcofacts: A Guide to Sensible Drinking,
Cardiff; Health Promotion Wales, 1997

Buzzed, by Cynthia Kuhn, Scott Swartzwelder
and Wilkie Wilson; New York and London: W.W.
Norton and Company, 1998

Drugs, by Anita Naik; part of Wise Guides
Series; London: Hodder Children's Books, 1997

Drugs and Violence in Sport, edited by
Craig Donnellan; Cambridge: Independence, 1995

Drugs Wise, by Melanie McFadyean;
Cambridge: Icon books, 1997

Taking Drugs Seriously, *A Parent's
Guide to Young People's Drug Use*, by
Julian Cohen and James Kay; London:
Thorsons, 1994

Teenage Alcoholism, by J Haskins,
Hawthorn Books, 1976

The Score: Facts about Drugs, HEA
leaflet; London: Health Education Authority, 1998

Glossary

abstinence
going without something totally, as with alcohol

alcoholism
a disease linked to a dependence on alcohol

alcopops
alcoholic drinks that taste sweet like soft drinks

BAC
Blood Alcohol Content, measured as the percentage of alcohol in the bloodstream

binge drinking
drinking a lot at one time

breathalyser
a device for measuring the amount of alcohol in someone's blood

brewing
producing alcoholic drinks such as beer by letting yeasts and sugars in a liquid turn to alcohol

cirrhosis
a disease of the liver caused by increased scar-tissue build-up

dependence, dependent
the physical or psychological craving for something

depressant
something that makes someone feel depressed

distillation
producing alcohol through a chemical process that involves evaporation and then condensation of alcohol; the operator is called the distiller

duty-free
having no taxes to pay (on, for example, alcohol)

ethanol
(ethyl alcohol) the chemical name for the alcohol in alcoholic drinks

ferment, fermentation
the naturally occurring change of sugar to alcohol in, for example, fruit juices

First World War
the war (1914-1918) between Germany, Austria and their allies against Britain, France and their allies

genetic
a characteristic or disease that is inherited from a parent

hallucinations
images that people think they see, but which are not really there

hallucinogenic
causing someone to see or hear things that are not there

hangover
a feeling of headache and sickness the morning after heavy drinking

Industrial Revolution
the period of rapid industrial development in the 18th and 19th centuries

infertility
inability to have children

inhibition
a feeling that holds someone back from expressing their feelings

intoxication
the state of losing physical and mental control after drinking

licensing
regulating the place and time of alcohol production, consumption and sale

microbreweries
small local breweries

off-licences
places in the UK that sell alcohol to be taken away and consumed elsewhere

peer pressure
the pressure from friends of the same age to behave in a certain way

pharmaceutical
the medical use of chemical science

physiological
relating to the way a living organism works

potent
having a powerful effect

pressure group
an organization that works together to change or influence laws

productivity
the efficiency of a company or a person

Prohibition
ban on alcohol imposed in the US after the First World War

rehabilitation
returning to a balanced and healthy way of life

Renaissance
the period in Europe from the late 15th to the mid-16th centuries when art and science blossomed

screening
a way of testing someone for a special condition

Second World War
the war (1939-1945) between Germany, Japan and their allies against Britain, the United States and their allies

taboo
something that is forbidden in a society

Temperance Movement
the 19th-century movement to ban alcohol

tolerance
the way in which the body learns to accept or expect more of a substance such as alcohol

toxic
poisonous

vineyards
plantations of grapevines where grapes (particularly for winemaking) are cultivated

vintages
special years when fine wines are produced

withdrawal
negative physical and mental effects from giving up something such as alcohol

Index

A absorption into the bloodstream 8, 10, 49
abstinence 47
addiction to alcohol 12-15
admitting to problem drinking 46-7
advertising 17, 26-7, 35, 36
alcohol abuse 14, 41
alcohol industry 17, 26-7, 34-7
alcohol poisoning 38, 46
alcohol-related illness 12, 13, 38-9, 49
alcoholism 4, 12, 14, 23, 28, 46, 49
alcopops 23, 33, 35, 36, 37, 48
anti-alcohol groups 20, 21
appetite loss 13
attractions of alcohol 4, 8, 17
availability 27, 30, 31, 35

B beers, lagers and ciders 6, 7, 18, 19, 23, 35
binge drinking 28, 32, 48
blood alcohol level 7, 40, 41
brain, effects on the 4, 6, 10, 13, 14, 23, 32, 40
brewing 7, 18

C cirrhosis of the liver 12, 13
counselling 45, 47, 48-9
crime 8, 38

D dependence 4, 12-15, 14, 24, 25, 32, 46, 49
depressant effect 10
depression 42
discount alcohol 31
disease, alcoholism as a 12, 46, 49
distillation 6, 7, 19
drink-driving 14, 36, 38, 40-1
drinking limits, suggested 11
Dutch courage 8

F family
    effects on the 14
    genetic factors 14, 33
    sensible drinking 28
fermentation 7, 18, 19
first drink 4, 49

G genetic factors 14, 33

H 'hair of the dog' 24
hallucinations 13
hangovers 24
health-care costs 38
high-profile drinkers 42-3
historical background 18-21

I infertility 33
information and advice 52-3
inhibitions, losing 8
injuries and death 8, 11, 12, 32, 38, 40, 42
intoxication 4, 11

J judgement, effects on 4, 14, 32
jumpiness 13

L licensing laws 20, 22, 40

M moderate drinking 4, 23, 28

O off-licences 17, 27, 31, 40

P panic attacks 14
peer pressure 27, 50
personal freedom and choice 26, 30, 49
physical co-ordination, loss of 4, 8
physiological processes 7, 8, 10
potency 6
pressure groups 36, 41
problem drinking 23, 24, 25, 28, 33, 42, 44-5, 46-7
Prohibition 20, 26
psychological dependence 14
public-awareness campaigns 20, 26, 36

R regular drinking 4
rehabilitation 14, 42
restrictions on sale and use of alcohol 4, 20, 22, 40
risk, groups at 32-3

S screening test 47
short-term effects 10-11
sleeplessness 13
social costs 38, 39
social relaxation 8, 10
social role of alcohol 4, 16-17, 22-3, 28
spirits 6, 7, 19-20, 21
sportspeople, alcohol and 17, 23, 42, 43

T taxes on alcohol 4, 30, 31, 34, 36
telephone helplines 50, 53
tolerance to alcohol 12-13, 32
toxic effects 13, 49
treatment 14, 42, 46-7
tremors 13

U unconsciousness 11
underage drinking 17, 27, 32, 41, 49
units of alcohol 11, 49

V violence 14, 32, 38

W wines 6, 7, 18, 19, 34-5
withdrawal symptoms 13
women
    alcohol absorbtion 8, 33
    alcohol-related health problems 33
    drinking during prgnancy 33
    risky drinking levels 25

Titles in the *Need to Know* series include:

Hardback   0 431 09779 8

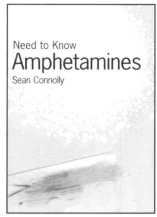

Hardback   0 431 09777 1

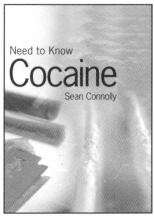

Hardback   0 431 09775 5

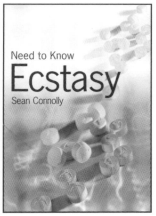

Hardback   0 431 09781 X

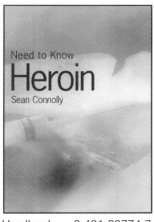

Hardback   0 431 09774 7

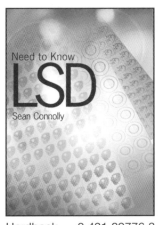

Hardback   0 431 09776 3

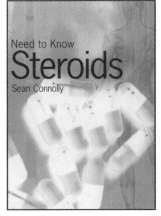

Hardback   0 431 09782 8

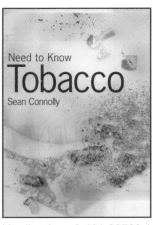

Hardback   0 431 09780 1

Find out about the other titles in this series on our website www.heinemann.co.uk/library